POSITIVITY

POSITIVITY

Confidence, Resilience, Motivation

Paul McKenna, DPhil

Edited by Kate McKenna

WELBECK

Published by Welbeck
An imprint of Welbeck Non-Fiction Limited,
part of Welbeck Publishing Group.
Based in London and Sydney.

Published by Welbeck in 2021

A CIP catalogue record for this book is available from the British Library

ISBN
Paperback – 9781787399600
eBook – 9781787399679

Typeset by Roger Walker

Printed in Great Britain by CPI Books, Chatham, Kent

10 9 8 7 6 5 4 3 2

The Forest Stewardship Council® is an international nongovernmental
organization that promotes environmentally appropriate, socially beneficial,
and economically viable management of the world's forests.
To learn more, visit www.fsc.org

www.welbeckpublishing.com

Important Notice

Do NOT use this book until you have read these pages.

You have in your hands one half of a system that will positively change your life. In order to use its transformative power, it is essential that you download the other half too – audio tracks which will focus your mind through visualisation and trance and set you on the pathway to success. This can be found at the paulmckenna.com website:

www.paulmckenna.com/downloads

The reason you are here, at this point in your life now with this book in your hands, is you want to embark on change. Just by picking up the book, you have sown the seeds of that transformation. This system will take you on to the next step. So, it's vital to understand this is not just a book to read, it is part of your life-changing solution. The book itself is the first essential element of the system and part one of your toolkit. The audio sessions that accompany it, are the second part. Both are just as important as each other. So, you must use both the book and the audio sessions together to achieve permanent, transformative success.

The audio sessions contain everything I would do if I were working with you personally, in the same room, one-on-one. They are simple, powerful psychological techniques and a hypnotic trance that strengthen the power of your unconscious mind to guide you towards success.

It is really easy to download onto your computer or smartphone. With just a few clicks, within minutes, you will have me there whenever you need, to help you make the changes you want in order to help you achieve your goals.

It's important to understand that intellectual knowledge is not the same as real, substantive change. So, you cannot expect lasting results if you only read this book. You must download and use the psychological techniques and guided hypnosis to achieve that.

During the hypnotic trance, which is contained in the audio session, your unconscious mind will become highly receptive to positive intentions. It is not the same as sleep – it is a wonderful state of deep relaxation like a daydream or meditation. Even though you are deeply relaxed, if for any reason you need to awaken, you will be able to do so, comfortably, calmly and with all the resources you need.

The audio sessions are not just essential, they are also enjoyable and rewarding. Many people use them over and over again to reinforce their new mind-set and enhance their success.

Ensure your success now. Go online to:

paulmckenna.com/downloads

Type in the following password to access your free audio downloads.

Password: Positivity123

Regularly use the sessions as directed in this book.

Enjoy the techniques and relax, knowing you are now on your way to lasting success!

Why will this system change your life for the better?

You hold in your hands not just a book, but a system that has taken years to develop and has been subject to rigorous testing. In the short amount of time that it will take you to read this, listen to the audio, and do the techniques, your life will change for the better. This toolkit allows you to tap into your hidden, transformative power – and that power is 'Positivity'. Connecting into it can transform every aspect of your life. Please don't just take my word for it. I am confident that the system that is this book, along with the audio techniques, is the most powerful psychological process I have made to date. It's written in a concise way to give you a fast-paced experience of positive change. As Albert Einstein said, "Everything should be made as simple as possible, but no simpler."

If you are feeling low, demoralized, anxious or unmotivated, if you are doing OK, but just need a boost, if you are doing well, but want to do even better, then the system that is contained in this book is for you. The techniques here are designed to help you keep calm under pressure, have more self-control, feel motivated and optimistic, choose your responses whilst maintaining perspective and feel powerfully confident. In other words, this system enables you to tap into a mindset, a way of thinking and behaving that I call 'Positivity'. That doesn't mean that you feel happy all the time even when bad things are occurring. If something terrible happens, it is normal, natural and OK to feel sad, angry or frightened, or a combination of all three but no-one wants to live in fear, anger or sadness all the time. As you use this system, your natural emotional default setting will be one of confidence, resilience and motivation. And as you become flooded with these positive feelings, and you embrace them, it will shape every aspect of your life from work to relationships and even your perception of your self.

This book and audio system uses the power of suggestion. This powerful technique is something which I have spent my life studying. Sometimes, people tell me they are not suggestible. So, I ask them, "What's your name?" And they reply with their name. So, next, I ask, "How do you know that?" And they usually say, "Because I just do." However, the reason they actually know is because somebody once told them that and it was reinforced over and over again. I ask them how they know the sky is blue and they say things like, "Because everybody knows." And once again, I say it was because somebody once suggested it to you. Everyone is suggestible, but that doesn't mean that everyone will respond to just any suggestion. A hypnotist is somebody who is good at getting people to respond to suggestions. By the time you have finished reading this book, you will have a useful understanding of the power of suggestion and how you can use it to enhance your life.

The scientific research shows that the fundamental building blocks of our beliefs about what we think about ourselves, the world and our lives are formed in the first seven years 'formative' years of our childhood. This is particularly true of experiences of strong emotional intensity, either positive or negative. Plato famously said, "Give me the boy before he's seven and I'll show you the man." These moments create a blueprint of who we believe we are and what we can and can't achieve in life and it's stored in the unconscious mind. One strong negative experience of public speaking early in life can create a belief that we are not a confident speaker. On the other hand, being complimented on something early in life, winning at a competition, being praised by an inspirational figure, or turning around a problematic situation, can form a belief that we are good at that particular thing, or even that we are talented. Sometimes, it can take an awful challenge that we survive, that helps form a belief that we are lucky or strong. Indeed, two people can experience similar events and yet have completely different beliefs about themselves and life as a result, because of the way in which they have interpreted that event. One might see themselves as 'lucky' – the other, as 'a victim'. One might view the cup as half full, the other as half empty. It's these decisions and thought processes we make at these formative moments which shape our potential to achieve what we want. They act like hypnotic suggestions that create an important template of our core self. All the techniques in this book are designed to help you choose the beliefs that you have about yourself and life and ultimately, the kind of life you want to have moving forward.

Often, there are a number of factors that result in a core belief being formed. As a schoolkid I was told I would never amount to anything in life and I remember feeling angry and thinking, 'I'll show you!' At any moment, you have a choice about how you interpret any given event. Whatever hand you have been dealt by life, you always have the power to change some aspect of it – either your viewpoint, your response to the event itself, or ultimately, the circumstances or outcome.

Of course, genetics plays a role in who we are as well, and the debate about how much our genetics and our environment shape us is ongoing and is usually agreed to be around a 50/50 split. However, recent research by Professor Bruce Lipton has shown that we can affect our genetics through our psychology, but to what extent is not truly known yet.

There is no doubt the scientific evidence shows that our early environment shapes us in ways that affect the rest of our lives. But what can be learned can be also unlearned. That means you can do something about it. The past does not need to define you if you don't want it to. Once I understood this, it led me to spend most of my life teaching people how to change the negative thought processes that stop them from fulfilling their potential, achieving something, or becoming who they want to be, for the better.

The reason why suggestions are powerful when they are made at a particular time in our formative years by an authority figure or at a moment of emotional intensity, is that they can shape thought processes that define our lives.

Those beliefs drive our thinking, feelings, habits and behaviours, so one of the objectives of this book and audio system is to help you to understand what the positive and negative suggestions are that you are operating out of all day long – not just suggestions from others, or those learned earlier in life, but also the suggestions we give to ourselves on a daily basis.

How amazing would it be if you could easily change any beliefs that have held you back, sabotaged you, or if you could improve your positive beliefs about yourself?

All day long, human beings give themselves suggestions in the form of an internal dialogue, a kind of self-hypnosis. We criticise the way we look or tell ourselves we really must do this or that and we do it without stopping to really notice if the suggestions are helpful or not. We navigate our way through life with a running commentary in our heads and this can be positive or negative, helpful or damaging. Many of us critique and analyse what others say to us, but we don't question our own internal voice. This system allows you to do that to liberate yourself from negativity or what is holding you back.

One of the main benefits to the system in this book is to give you the power to literally become your own self-hypnotist, so you can do more than just give yourself positive suggestions, you can use the power of your creative imagination to liberate yourself from negative mind-sets that hold you back, solve problems and create a better future.

One of the biggest myths about the power of suggestion

Back in the 1950s, there was a lot of controversy surrounding subliminal advertising when a market researcher named James Vicary inserted the words "Eat Popcorn" and "Drink Coca-Cola" into a movie. The words appeared for a single frame – allegedly long enough for the unconscious to pick up, but too short for the viewer to be aware of it. The subliminal ads supposedly created an increase in Coca-Cola and popcorn sales in the cinema, but Vicary's results turned out to be a hoax.

However, subliminal advertising was banned soon after in the US as a result. Of course, we can be aware of things that are outside our conscious awareness – a mother can awaken in the middle of the night if she hears her baby cry or we can be at a social gathering and somebody says our name over the other side of the room and we suddenly tune in and hear it – but this does not mean that just because we receive a message outside of our conscious awareness, we will always act upon it.

Perhaps the best example of the debunking of the effectiveness of subliminal suggestions comes in two forms – firstly, why is it not possible to learn a language subliminally? Secondly, by a remarkable experiment carried out by Dr Richard Bandler where he recorded a cassette for a control group with subliminal suggestions on it such as, 'You feel unhappy', or 'Life is terrible', or, 'Everything feels bad'. As he gave the cassette to each member of the control group, he told them in a meaningful way that the cassette contained positive suggestions that would make them feel good and their lives amazing. One month later, every single member of the control group reported that they were happier, more optimistic, and had a wonderful life. This makes a really important point – that one **well-delivered, congruent, conscious suggestion** is better than 100,000 subliminal ones. In other words, it's not just the suggestion, but *the way in which it's given* and *by whom it's given*.

What makes this system work so well?

I am often asked or even studied by researchers to understand why I am an effective hypnotist. I believe it's because my life is about constantly giving positive suggestions to people, but in different ways. Sometimes these take a very simple form such as a congruent conscious suggestion when I tell someone at just the right moment with the force of my personality, 'You will stop smoking', or, 'You will become totally confident', or, 'You will be a happier person for the rest of your life.' Other times, I use a gentle avalanche of continual indirect suggestions embedded in what appears to be just a conversation where I tell stories that have layers of meaning for someone's unconscious mind. I also like to use a sophisticated system of holographic suggestions in the form of a trance, where I communicate with the right brain and left brain – the whole mind. The left brain is synonymous with logic, linear and process. The right brain is synonymous with emotion and abstract. That's why I will be giving your left brain process instructions and I'll be talking to your right brain through metaphor and imagery. Combining these two systems of communication is a sophisticated way to talk to your whole brain.

I have made a trance that comes with this book to help you programme your mind to reduce stress, increase your confidence, resilience, motivation and happiness using a beautiful matrix of suggestions that elicit your creative possibilities and generate positive resourceful states within you.

This is not just another motivational book. I want to help you using modern scientific techniques, such as NLP (Neuro-Linguistic Programming) to transform your mindset to view the world through positive perceptual filters that can help you to see opportunities and discover new ways that empower you. I'm using all of my years of experience as a hypnotist and Neuro-Linguistic Programmer to build a system that means that no matter whether or not you believe a single word I say, simply the act of reading these words and listening to the audio techniques will help you to feel more optimistic and have a better life.

Everything that I would do in a personal session to enhance your positivity if we were sat together in my study, I am going to do with you now.

The Power of Habit

Nearly half of what we do every day is a result of habits. We don't think to ourselves, 'Shall I brush my teeth this morning?' or 'Shall I bother to get dressed before I leave the house?'. You just do it because of the power of your habits.

When I am asked, "How do you break a habit?" The answer is that you don't break a habit, you replace it with another habit until the new one takes hold.

This is where visualisation, hypnosis and the power of the human imagination is so powerful. Champion athletes do something called 'mental rehearsal' – they imagine running a race, beating an opponent and winning over-and-over again until it becomes second nature, so they are literally hard-wired in their mind and muscle memory to succeed.

Basketball legend Michael Jordan demonstrated this years ago when he was making a TV commercial where he had to throw the ball near to the basket but miss the shot for comedic purposes. However, he had to take the shot 7 times, because he kept getting the ball in by accident. He's hard-wired to succeed. You are going to practise going into similar peak states of performance and imagine succeeding over-and-over again as you do the techniques in this system.

We are going to rehearse having success, happiness, resilience, motivation and confidence in life in your mind until they become second nature for you. Your new default position will be as an even happier, more amazing person than you are right now.

All my books, APPS or online courses either focus on solving problems or creating aspiration and achieving a wonderful life. This book is about combining both. There are lots of techniques that we are about to do that will help you create powerful, lasting change.

The pandemic has given me a unique opportunity over the last couple of years to have worked with tens of thousands of people – some one-to-one and others in large groups via video link to test this system repeatedly. So, please don't just read this book, do the techniques, download the audio versions and let me help you programme your mind for a happier, more successful life.

This book is written in a particular style. Whereas before, I had to spend time convincing, explaining and reassuring people before I did a life-changing technique, when I work with people these days, they almost always just want to cut to the chase and that's the beauty of this book and audio system. We get straight on with an avalanche of positive techniques that you are going to be using to transform your thinking and behaviours for your new, positive future.

Why the techniques in this book are different from traditional therapy...

In recent years, there's been a revolution in the world of human potential. In the same way that a mobile phone in the 1980s was the size of a brick and all you could do was make phone calls on it, nowadays, a mobile phone is the size of a bar of chocolate and it's actually a super-computer. It has your office and your music on it, you can access all the information about just about anything from the web, make video conference calls in real time and so much more.

In the same way, psychological technology has made quantum leaps in the last few decades. For example, it used to take around six months to cure a phobia using traditional desensitisation, but recent breakthroughs by modern psychologists now mean that lifelong problems such as phobias can be cured in minutes. Often, I work with people who have been labelled 'incurable' and yet I am able to treat them successfully, not because I possess some magic power, but because new psychological technology means that we now have a better understanding of the structure of human thinking and behaviour. A new age of human potential is upon us!

There are definitely some benefits to talking therapies – it can be helpful to get something off your chest and to post-rationalise something traumatic from the past, but generally, I don't find just trying to 'talk things through', to be as effective an approach to solving all of life's psychological and behavioural problems as the modern techniques that we are about to use in this system.

For example, I have met people who've been in therapy for decades and can *explain* their problems – often in the same language as a psychologist – but it hasn't made any difference to their dysfunctional behaviour whatsoever. Many traditional talking therapies are based on the idea that *understanding* your issue provides a cure – that talking through the most upsetting experiences of your past means you will eventually reach a realisation about why you do the things you do that are dysfunctional.

Whilst it is true that formative experiences early in life shape us, just remembering them will not automatically change the way we think and act in the future. The whole premise that knowing intellectually why you developed a destructive behaviour will suddenly stop you from doing it in future and set you free is just not the case. If it was, all we would ever need to do is think back to the first time we did something dysfunctional, realise why we did it and it would magically just stop. This obsession with digging into a person's past to discover the root to dysfunction can mean re-living traumatic memories over-and-over again, which can actually leave the patient feeling a lot worse and of course the therapist a lot richer. Our objective is to *re-code* the way we interpret things from the past, so that we're no longer bothered by them, but can keep all the learning from the experience without the dysfunctional effect.

The main reason for dysfunctional behaviours is because the unconscious mind is not logical, but purposeful – all the logical arguments make no difference if the purpose is survival. No amount of logic about how safe an aeroplane is will stop a phobic feeling frightened. For example, travelling by plane is approximately 100 times safer than in a car, or you are more likely to be injured in a trouser-related incident than be injured in a plane, but knowing that will not stop the mind from creating states of fear in a phobic person, because its purpose is trying to protect you. As a child, I was bitten by a dog and for years I had a phobia of all dogs, no matter what size they were or how friendly they seemed. My mind produced massive fear because the purpose was protection, even if it was a tiny, friendly dog.

I once worked with an entrepreneur who found that whenever he started to get successful, he would find a way to sabotage what he was doing, no matter how hard he tried not to. It turned out that as a child he had said to his mother that when he grew up, he wanted to be a very successful businessman and his mother replied, "You don't want that, son, those kinds of people have heart attacks." That casual, throwaway phrase had stuck, and shaped his future. Obviously, there is no logic in that statement, but because it was said by an authority figure to a child at an impressionable age, it became embedded into his unconscious mind with the power of a hypnotic suggestion. His unconscious mind was not thinking logically, but with its prime purpose of survival, it did everything it could to stop him becoming successful, with the intention of keeping him alive.

That's why the best way to cure such a problem is to go to the structure of a person's thinking – the sequence of pictures and sounds in the mind that create feelings and are the building blocks of beliefs. By changing them, the thoughts de-link from the feelings and suddenly aeroplanes, or dogs, or business success, no longer create fear.

Unfortunately, the field of psychology has been obsessed with labelling people's problems, so that a drug can be prescribed, and this has been going on for more than a hundred years. It's not just that this model is good for business, this obsession with looking at how people are broken and labelling them is part of the culture that emerged from the work of Sigmund Freud, the father of psychoanalysis. Like many therapists these days, I have no regard for the work of Freud and consider many of his 'theories' to have been counter-productive to people's lives.

Some years ago, I met a Freudian analysist and very early on in the conversation, she asked me why I hated myself. I replied that I wasn't aware that I did and indeed how did she know that I hated myself? She replied, "Because we all hate ourselves." I suggested that we find a phobic and see which one of us could cure them. She said that the point of Freudian analysis is not to 'cure' people, but to help them understand *why* they are phobic. I explained why I thought that was unhelpful by a simple metaphor – if I take my car to the garage and ask them to fix it and they say we can't do that, but we can tell you *why* your car is broken, it's not going to be much use.

The DSM (Diagnostic and Statistical Manual of Mental Disorders) now has hundreds of ways of describing people as broken and in some cases, incurable and whilst it's entirely necessary to diagnose problems, it seems to me a shame there isn't equally an emphasis on how to direct people towards mental wellness, which isn't just pharmaceutical. In recent years, a new branch of psychology has developed from the work of Martin Seligman and others called 'Positive Psychology.' This is a relatively new branch of psychology that shifts the focus from what is clinically wrong with a person, to that of wellbeing and what is satisfying for example, meaning, pleasure, engagement, positive relationships, accomplishment, etc.

So, after more than a hundred years, the field of psychology is shifting away from constantly looking at how everyone might be broken and now creating models of functionality to move towards.

For me, personally, behavioural modelling is where the most exciting developments are taking place. It's a process of codifying the patterns of thinking and behaviour of somebody who is dysfunctional, so we can change them, or the process of codifying the patterns of thinking and behaviour of somebody who is a model of excellence, so these patterns can be subsequently to be taught to anyone. In other words, if somebody has a dysfunctional set of strategies, by understanding the structure of them, it becomes easy to replace them with new functional ones. The difference between this and traditional analytical understanding is that this is about understanding **how** you do something and how in future you can take control of it and change it, whereas analytical therapies often concentrate on understanding **why** you do something, but not necessarily providing you with a solution as to how to change it.

So, let's look at *how* you do something. For example, how do people make themselves feel compelled to drink alcohol? They might picture a glass with ice cubes clinking and the sound of alcohol pouring into the glass, and then imagine the first sip, the taste, the feeling and the sequence of sounds and pictures in their minds.

An analyst will want to know *why* somebody drinks too much. Possibly, it will be a trauma in the past, but just knowing it's a trauma and going back and recalling that trauma, over-and-over again, is very unlikely to change the behaviour in future.

However, by *re-coding* the trauma or event and the way the brain processes it, *will* change behaviours. Recognising the steps that lead you to a certain behaviour and interrupting that pattern and putting another pattern in place will give you the tools to modify whatever behaviour you would like to change.

Also, if somebody is exceptional at something, such as therapy, sales, maths, athletics, memorizing information, art, fighting, comedy, presenting, etc, by learning their strategies, it's possible to codify them and teach them to others in a fraction of the time it would normally take to master that talent.

So, this book is not just another bunch of theories, it's a collection of techniques and strategies created from studying highly-functional and successful people. As you practise them, your life will change immeasurably for the better and you will be liberated from what holds you back.

Don't be too surprised at how soon you start to notice changes...

Please do not underestimate what we are about to do. This is not just a book on feeling good or another self-help book full of soundbite wisdom that makes a jolly read or something to pass the time that you pick up at the airport. It is not a series of 'mind tricks.' As you read these words, which are written in a special hypnotic language that create a specific sequence in your thoughts, and you practise the audio techniques, you will train your brain to make yourself even better than you had ever dreamed possible before. In athletics, the difference between a medal and an 'also ran' is 1% – this system will give you far more than the 1%. You hold in your hands the difference between a mediocre life and a truly happy and successful one.

Last year, a friend of mine who is also a therapist contacted me. He was working with a patient who had lost his confidence, his direction and his mojo. He called me, because during one of their sessions, his patient said, "I need a hypnotist. I need someone to put a suggestion in my mind so that I believe in myself again." Many years earlier in his life, he'd been struggling, and he'd been to see a local hypnotist who'd put him in a trance and told him to believe in himself. It didn't just make him confident – he became hugely successful. So, I did just that, I hypnotised this extraordinary man and got him to remember times in his life that he'd succeeded and imagined what he would look like if he was totally confident, his ultimate self, how he would stand, smile, how his voice would sound and to picture the light shining behind his eyes. I then told him to step into that ultimate self and become him, like a method actor, and that was it. He was back!

Sometimes, one hypnotic process is all it takes, however, sometimes it needs to be re-enforced. It doesn't matter how many times you listen to the hypnotic trance that comes with this book or read the pages that are filled with suggestions to make you more confident, resilient and happier because even as your eyes scan these words and your amazing mind makes sense of what I am saying, the suggestions that help you most are going into your unconscious mind and your life is about to get a lot better.

This book is in four sections because the key to living in a state of positivity, for most of the time, is achieved by four things:

Reducing stress – This is because when we are in a state of excessive stress and are continually looking for threats, we do not have enough bandwidth for other kinds of positive thoughts and feelings.

So, the first section is on reducing stress.

The second section is on:

Increasing confidence – Self-belief and confidence are positive states of mind and body where we usually make good decisions and are in the flow of life where we can maximise opportunities and potential.

The third section is on:

Resilience – This is more than just being able to tough it out when challenges arise. Resilience is about adaptability, creativity and resourceful thinking.

The final section is on:

Motivation – Once we are feeling confident and resilient, we need to decide what it is that's important in life and point ourselves in that direction. Through a process of getting clear about what's really important to us, we can then find massive motivation to go for what it is that we truly want.

Section 1
Reducing Stress & Creating Calm

One of the most important principles that you can take away from this book is simply that:

There are only two ways to feel good or feel bad about anything:

either remembering something good or bad that happened, or imagining something good or bad that could happen.

When we recall something or imagine something, we create movies in our mind – often with a soundtrack – so put simply, it's the internal pictures and the sounds that create our feelings from moment to moment. Say, for example, we get invited to a party and we instantly imagine standing alone in the kitchen not knowing anybody, we get an uncomfortable feeling and decide not to go. However, if we make a movie of ourselves interacting with fun people, laughing and relaxed, we get a good feeling and that leads to a different decision. All day long, we navigate our way through life with the movies we make in our minds and the things we say to ourselves.

In the first section of this book, we are going to discover how it is that that we can either create or reduce unnecessary stress in our lives through the pictures and the sounds that we make in our imagination. Once we have more control over our thoughts and feelings, we have control over our choices and behaviours and ultimately control over our lives. Obviously, we can't control everything that ever happens to us in life, but we have a big say in how we think and feel about them.

Unfortunately, many people don't know how to have control over how they feel and behave and ultimately the results they get. As I have already mentioned, many of the things they do each day are just habits.

I have noticed that far too many people spend too much of their lives running negative movies in their mind to motivate themselves – constantly *moving away* from fear rather than *towards* happiness is not a very enjoyable way to live life. As you use this system, you are going to train your brain to feel good more of the time and move towards what you really want.

If I could give people one gift from all the techniques that I have, it would be for them to be able to have more control over their mind and body so that they weren't unnecessarily stressed. Psychologists refer to thinking about all the worst things that could possibly happen to us as 'catastrophising' – worrying about things that will never happen, preparing for emergencies that are never going to occur and getting worked up about imaginary threats, instead of focusing on the moment and the reality. Not only is this exhausting, but it doesn't allow for us to be creative, optimistic and happy. If you are in a state of stress, you are looking for threats everywhere. As Mark Twain famously said, "I've lived through some terrible things in my life – some of which actually happened." Particularly since the pandemic, many people understandably have trained themselves to continually think about worst case scenarios.

The body's stress response mechanism works like a car alarm. If a threat is detected or perceived, the internal alarm system lets us know something is wrong by creating a change in our body chemistry, producing adrenaline and cortisol. We then feel alert and get a burst of fear or anger. In an extreme situation, we experience the 'fight or flight' response which dates back to when we were cave people and had to either fight a wild animal or run away.

However, the stress response is not just triggered when there is a physical threat to ourselves, but also a threat to our ego. So, if there is a chance of us looking bad – say giving a presentation – then the stress response is triggered. These things may not seem like real 'threats', but your nervous system can't tell the difference between a physical threat and an imagined threat to your ego.

In modern life, there are lots of minor stresses every day – an argument, a traffic jam, running late, etc, and all these small threats add up. So, you don't have to have a gun to your head to experience lots of stress if you have accumulated many small stresses throughout the day.

However, how we interpret things makes all the difference. The father of stress research Dr Hans Selye famously said:

"It's not the event, but rather our interpretation of it that causes our emotional reaction."

Using this system means your perception and interpretation of events that used to stress you changes, and you will begin to respond differently, have more bandwidth in your thinking for resilience and creativity in solving problems which ultimately leads to more positive results in life. The better you feel, the more you can see the world as it is, rather than how you fear it might be.

Thought experiments...

Albert Einstein, one of the most creative thinkers of all time, used to do what he called 'thought experiments.' These were simple visualisation exercises that helped him understand possibilities.

So, let's do our first thought experiment – because it's not just *what* we think about, but the *way* we think about it that's important. At school, we are taught *what* to think, but we are not taught *how* to think. So, here's our first experiment:

1. Make yourself comfortable and remember a time that you felt very good. Return to that memory like you're back there again now. See what you saw... hear what you heard... and feel how good you felt. Make the colours rich, bright and bold... the sounds loud and feelings strong. Right now, you should be feeling really good.

2. Next, I'd like you to think about a mildly uncomfortable memory – maybe a time when you had an argument, or you felt disappointed or upset. And when you think about that time now... I would like you to step out of the memory, step out of yourself and look at yourself as though the event is happening to somebody else. Next, drain all the colour out of that event and make it black and white. And then gently fade it out. Right now, you should be feeling significantly less upset.

What we're learning here is a very important principle. Whenever we are **inside** a memory it will have much **greater emotional intensity** than when we are **outside** of it. So, put simply, one of the processes we are going to do during this system is stepping into good times and stepping out of bad times. This will re-code the general landscape of our thinking to make us more optimistic, and free from any uncomfortable past experiences. We will keep all the learnings of the bad things that have happened to us in life, but just not be troubled by them anymore.

From working with people such as soldiers and paramedics who have been through extremely traumatic experiences, some are functional, and some were not. The ones that were functional are those that have coded their experiences in a way that means they are not in a permanent state of upset. They can remember something terrible happened and have kept the learnings they needed from it. Those that are dysfunctional are sadly constantly re-living the events that are long over, again and again, in a continual survival mode. In some ways, one of the best things about the past is that it's over.

So many of us have a negative internal voice – running self-destructive messages that hold us back. From looking in the mirror and hearing the dialogue of 'your bum looks big in that', to the confidence-chipping inner voice of 'I can't', it's time to stop that negative bad talk and that's a key part of learning the power of internal positivity.

However, it's not just *what* you say to yourself, it's also *how* you say it. I'd like you to consider how the world sounds when you're stressed. What does your internal dialogue sound like? Is it worried, or anxious? Do you speak calmly to yourself? Or do you sound frightened or concerned? So, if we are talking to ourselves inside our mind in a way that is stressed and frightened, it will naturally make us feel more stressed.

I'd like you to tap into your inner voice, so, let's try another thought experiment.

1. I'd now like you to talk to yourself inside your mind now in a very gentle, calm way. With your internal dialogue, I'd like you to use the same tone of voice that you'd use to tell a bedtime story.

2. And say something really calming such as, 'All is well. All is well.' And notice how that feels.

So, as well as what we say to ourselves inside our minds all day long, **the way we say it is very important.**

Progressive relaxation...

It's now time to do our first technique. We're going to imagine ourselves more and more relaxed. As you step, or float into that more relaxed self, you are going to increase the level of relaxation you feel. You will also talk to yourself calmly inside your mind and in doing so, create a profoundly relaxed state of mind and body simply by using the power of your imagination.

Once you learn to put yourself into a deep state of relaxation at will, you have real power. So, by practising this technique several times, you will have mastery over an important part of yourself and your life.

Please read through this exercise before you do it. If you like, you can download the audio version, so I can walk you through each step.

1. Close your eyes and imagine another 'you', one that is twice as relaxed as you are right now.

2. Imagine floating over and into that more relaxed you. See through the eyes of your more relaxed self, hear the through the ears of your more relaxed self and feel this deeper relaxation.

3. Next, imagine another you, one that is twice as relaxed as you are right now.

4. Imagine floating over and into that more relaxed you. See through the eyes of your more relaxed self, hear the through the ears of your more relaxed self and feel this deeper relaxation.

5. From this place, imagine another you, one that is even more as relaxed as you are right now.

6. Imagine floating over and into that even more relaxed you. See through the eyes of your more relaxed self, hear through

the ears of your more relaxed self and feel this deeper relaxation.

7. Pause for a little, while you notice the feelings and then, if you wish, repeat it. Continue imagining a more relaxed you and floating into it, until you are totally relaxed.

8. Stay with this feeling for as long as you wish. You will be able to return to full, waking consciousness, refreshed and alert, as soon as you are ready.

Havening – the biggest psychological breakthrough of the 21st century

In recent years, a new field of therapy called 'psycho-sensory' has developed that has become very popular – mainly because the results are so fast and astounding. There are a number of these psycho-sensory techniques – TFT (Thought Field Therapy), EMDR (Eye Movement Desensitization and Reprocessing) and the like – however, I personally find Havening to be the most powerful of all of them.

Psycho-sensory techniques work by the use of specific eye movements, the touch of certain parts of the body and visualisations. They are deceptively simple, and originally disregarded by some of the conventional psychiatric community, but the results speak for themselves. These techniques are now widely used successfully by the military and the emergency services, first responders and leading clinicians worldwide in the treatment of PTSD, stress, pain and a host of other disorders.

Havening Therapy was created by my friend Ronald Ruden MD. Ph.D. Scientific studies have shown that it is amazingly effective at reducing sadness, reducing stress and trauma.

Dr Ruden's work has been hailed as a remarkable breakthrough. He discovered that patterns of repeated touch to parts of the body combined with specific eye movements and visualisations have a rapid, reliable and predictable effect on our feelings by producing more delta waves in the brain (delta waves are associated with the deepest levels of relaxation and restorative sleep).

His years of research have created a significant advance in the treatment of many 'incurable' problems. The patterns of touch used in Havening are what enable a mother to comfort her baby as they are hard-wired into every infant. Havening combines these deep-rooted patterns of reassurance with sequences to break down the associations that triggered unhappy or uncomfortable feelings. As a result, in just a few minutes, we can now reduce the intensity of an emotion or feeling of unhappiness and establish calm.

This technique is not merely a distraction. Studies have shown that when we use the Havening Technique, we reduce stress chemicals in our body and produce states of relaxation and calm. We also change the way our brain processes thoughts and feelings. The effect of the specific sequence I will share with you is to reset the way that your brain interprets and responds to stress. Over time, this actually alters the neural pathways in your brain.

A Safe Haven

Please read through the following exercise before you do it. You should practise this sequence of eye movements, body touches and visualisations several times until you know it off by heart. Then you will be able to use it any time you need to get rid of unhappy feelings and swiftly feel calm and relaxed. If you would like me to guide you through it personally, you can download the audio recording.

1. Pay attention to any stress or traumatic memory you wish to remove and notice what it looks like in your imagination and how stressful it feels. Now, rate its strength on a scale of 1-10, where 10 is the most powerful and 1 is the least powerful. This is important as it lets you measure how much you are reducing it.

2. Now, clear your mind, or just think about or imagine something nice.

3. Now, cross your arms, place your hands on the tops of your shoulders and close your eyes.

4. Now, stroke your hands down the sides of your arms from the top of your shoulders down to your elbows, and keep doing this downward stroking motion, again and again, throughout this process.

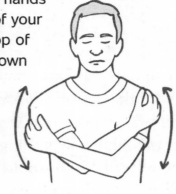

5. As you carry on stroking the sides of your arms, imagine you are walking on a beautiful beach, with each footstep you take in the sand, count out loud from 1 to 20. 1, 2, 3...

6. Now, keeping your head still, whilst continuing to stroke your arms, move your eyes laterally to the left and laterally to the right ten times.

7. Still stroking the sides of your arms, imagine you are walking outside in a beautiful garden, with each footstep you take in the grass, count out loud from 1 to 20. 1, 2, 3...

8. Now, open your eyes and check on your scale from 1 to 10, how much lower the number of the stress feeling is now.

If it is way down the bottom of the scale, congratulations – you have personally changed your feelings. If you think that the stress feeling is not yet reduced enough, just repeat the Havening sequence until it is reduced as far as you want.

Many people experience remarkable positive changes immediately after a Havening session, however even if you are one of those people, I recommend that you do this Havening exercise regularly.

Emotional Intelligence

Even though some of our feelings may be uncomfortable, all of our feelings are part of our emotional intelligence – their purpose is to let us know that we need to pay attention to something. When something makes us happy, it lets us know we feel good, so we seek more of it. However, there are other feelings that are not so comfortable, but very necessary in order to protect us and keep us in the natural balance of life. Let's consider the uncomfortable feelings that are not just necessary, but part of our overall intelligence.

Fear

Fear is really just a warning that something bad *could* happen, so pay attention and be prepared. If you feel that you are fully prepared, or if you are experiencing fear in a situation where you normally feel comfortable, it could be a genuine warning of physical danger. For example, if I am about to cross the road and a bus is coming towards me quite close, then I need a burst of fear to pull me back and keep me alive.

Anger

Anger is usually a sign that one of our standards or boundaries has been violated, either by ourselves or by someone else. The message is to either take action for what we believe is right or in some cases, to accept the things we cannot change. For example, if someone is rude to us, the anger motivates us to tell them to stop it, or for us to withdraw from the situation.

Frustration

Frustration is in the same family as anger. It arises when we're not achieving the level of results that we believe we should. The message is usually to get us to re-evaluate and motivate us to achieve the goal.

Guilt

Guilt tends to come about whenever we are not living up to one of our own standards. Guilt's message is very simple – don't do it again and do what needs to be done to put it right! For example, if in the heat of a discussion I say something mean-spirited, the feeling of guilt helps me to make an effort to repair the relationship.

Sadness

Sadness is the result of feeling that something is missing from our lives, either because we've lost it or we've lost touch with it. The underlying message is both to appreciate what we've lost and to be grateful for what we still have. In some cases, the message may be to fight to get it back, as in the case of a 'lost love'. However, without some sadness in life, it's impossible to have any sense of value, because how can you know

happiness without having experienced some
sadness?

None of the above feelings are comfortable,
but they are essential in keeping us alive and
functional. However, we certainly don't want to
live in these feelings all the time. That's why the
next technique is so important in re-calibrating
our emotions into the eco-system of our feelings
– our emotional intelligence. It's very important
to have a full dynamic range of emotions, but not
to be ruled by ones that leave us feeling upset or
stuck in a moment too often.

Don't be too surprised by the power of the
process we are about to do. I have seen people
who have been consumed by rage or fear for
years, suddenly find peace. You will still have
all of your ability to protect yourself, all of your
emotional intelligence, but you will find that
your feelings will signal to you in ways that
guide you rather than rule you. Indeed, you will
become a master of your emotions.

The Apex Technique

This technique is inspired from the work of my friend, the brilliant Zen Master Genpo Roshi.

Read the exercise all the way through so that you understand it before starting. Or if you'd like to download the audio version of this technique, I will walk you through each step.

1. Place your hands out in front of you with your palms turned up.

2. Next, let yourself focus on the feeling that is bothering you, whatever it is. It could be a fear, anger, or something else.

3. As you notice it, ask if there is anything that feeling would wish to say to you. If there is, make a note of it – if there is not, that is absolutely fine, too.

4. Now imagine holding the feeling in your left hand, in front of you and get in touch with it.

5. Now I'd like you to think of the opposite of that feeling – for example, peace, calm, comfort.

6. Bring that opposite feeling to mind – peace, calm, comfort – and notice how it feels.

7. Now imagine placing that opposite, positive feeling in your right hand, in front of you.

8. Now move your attention up to a few inches above your head and keeping your attention in that position now experience both feelings at the same time.

PLACE ATTENTION HERE

9. Continue to feel the two emotions simultaneously with your attention above your head. As you do that, your emotional system will re-calibrate so that you can experience that difficult emotion at a lower level as it re-integrates into your emotional intelligence.

You should now be feeling significantly calmer with more emotional equilibrium when you think about things that were challenging. Practise these techniques as often as you feel you need to, until they become second nature. Now that we've reduced the stress, it's time to increase your confidence!

In a Nutshell

- Stress is caused by over-stimulating the mind and body's protection mechanism.

- It's not what happens to us, but the way we choose to perceive it, that creates stress.

- Learning to relax ourselves naturally is a powerful stress-reducing habit.

- Use The Havening Technique regularly to reduce stress.

- Your emotions are part of your intelligence – when they are overwhelming, using the Apex Technique will re-set them so you keep the benefit of the message without feeling too stressed.

Section 2

Instant Confidence & Self-Belief

My definition of confidence is 'being comfortable in your own skin – authentic and natural.' About 20 years ago, I wrote a book on Confidence and when I told people what I was writing, some people said things like, "Oh, great, a training manuals for arseholes!" That's because some people have the assumption that confident people are full-on, in your face, full of themselves and arrogant. However, as far as I'm concerned, those people are very *un*-confident – they are trying too hard and overcompensating. Truly confident people are authentically themselves – they don't need to pretend to be something they are not – they feel perfectly good enough as they are.

Since the pandemic, many people have experienced uncertainty. In surveys into what people fear most, 'the unknown' is usually in the top ten, sometimes even higher than death. So, confidence and self-belief are what many people really need right now and this chapter is all about giving you inner self-confidence – a strong belief in yourself and your abilities to handle life's challenges.

Over the years, I have had the opportunity to work with some of the highest achievers in the world of sports, business, the arts, politics and other fields and whilst I am convinced that confidence is ultimately a state of mind and body, it's also a habit – a habit that can be learned and turned on at will. By the time you have read this section and practised the techniques, you will be able to tap into your natural confidence whenever you want. Imagine the power that will give you – being able to walk into a meeting, give a presentation, or handle a challenging situation in a state of total self-confidence.

It never ceases to amaze me how someone can go from a state of complete terror to one of complete conviction in just moments with the aid of a few simple techniques. For example, some Olympic athletes, who have trained for an event for years, walk out into a stadium with a billion people watching them on TV and suddenly they lack confidence, and their performance suffers. Others have trained not only their bodies, but their minds, to go into a peak state of performance – they call it being 'in the zone'. Musicians refer to it as being 'in the groove' and psychologists call it being 'in flow' – a peak state of performance where you are in a state of total focus, you move and express yourself perfectly and nothing else in the world matters because you are totally in the moment.

The most famous recent example of this happening is 18-year-old Emma Raducanu at the US Open – even when she cut her knee on the match point, forcing play to stop, she stayed in the zone and walked into the history books. She'd taken the tough lesson of having to retire from Wimbledon earlier in the year with breathing difficulties and turned it into a positive. She said in an interview: "I think Wimbledon was an extremely positive experience. I learned so much about my game and what it takes to perform at the top". There are countless other examples in sport of overcoming the odds to success by getting "in the zone"– Dennis Taylor lost the first seven frames of the world snooker in 1985 but went on to beat Steve Davis, Tiger Woods won the Masters 11 years after his last major win and in 1981 Bob Champion and Aldaniti won the Grand National after the jockey battled back from cancer while his mount had suffered three serious leg injuries that almost resulted in the horse being put down.

I am going to show you how to turn that on whenever you like and that will in turn help you to have the life you want.

This type of confidence is not something that some people are born with, and others will never attain – it is the inevitable result of taking a few daily actions on a consistent basis. It is a process that you have already begun doing simply by picking up this book.

Stop for a moment and vividly imagine how your life would be if you were already naturally confident right now – at ease with yourself and whatever is going on around you:

- How would your posture be?

- How would your voice sound?

- What kinds of things would you be saying to yourself?

- What would you picture in your mind?

If you actually took the time to imagine any of these things, chances are you are already feeling more confident than you were just a few short moments ago. The reason is that the human nervous system doesn't know the difference between a real and a vividly-imagined experience, so when we imagine scary things, it makes us scared, when we imagine relaxing things we feel relaxed.

But as you will soon learn, confidence is much more than just a positive feeling in your body – it's an attitude and approach to life that leads to success, motivation and new possibilities!

Let's do a technique now to make you more confident.

Read the exercise through first before starting, so
you understand each step, or if you want me to
talk you through it, you can download the audio
version.

The Gradual Confidence Booster

1. Imagine a slightly more confident 'you'
    sitting or standing in front of you.

2. Now, I'd like you to imagine stepping in
    to that more confident you. See through
    their eyes, hear through their ears and
    feel the feelings of your more confident
    self.

3. Notice that right in front of you is an
    even more confident you – sitting or
    standing a little bit taller, a look of
    slightly more self-belief behind their
    eyes and emanating a little bit of extra
    charisma.

4. Now step into this more confident self
    and then notice that in front of you is an
    even more confident self – more passion,
    more power, more ease, more comfort.

> 5. Then again, imagine an *even more* confident you sitting or standing in front of you.
>
> 6. And step into that more confident you. Feel your confidence overflowing! Be sure to notice how you are using your body – how you are breathing, the expression on your face, and the light in your eyes.

A lot of people think that being confident means doing some important act like speaking in a massive auditorium or making a huge business decision. Whereas the confidence people experience in everyday life can be something as simple as shopping in a supermarket. There's no worry present – just a decisive, simple, effortless, determined act of picking out the items that you want. That, by definition, is a form of confidence.

The word 'confidence' itself comes from Latin *'confidentia',* from *'confidere'* which means 'to have full trust.'

Some people tell me that they find it difficult to imagine themselves as more confident, in which case, we need to simply borrow from the confidence of others. This is how human beings naturally learn. For example, one of the reasons human beings find it relatively easy to learn to drive a car is because for years most people have sat behind someone driving and have watched how it was done and in their minds, they can put themselves in the place of the driver.

So, let's do a technique where we borrow from the confidence of someone who is extremely confident. It can be a famous person, or it can be your Aunt Gladys – it doesn't matter, as long as the person you choose is someone you think of as a confident person.

Read through the entire technique first or download the audio version and I will talk you through each step.

Borrowing from a Confident Role Model

1. Think of someone whose confidence and charisma you wish to emulate.

2. Think of a time when they exhibited the skill you wish to learn.

3. Now, run through that memory of your role model performing that particular skill. Do this several times. If it helps, do it once in slow motion.

4. Now, go over to your role model and float into their body, and synchronize with their posture, stand or sit exactly the way they do. Pull the same expression they do. See through their eyes, hear through their ears and feel how confident they feel.

5. Now run through the memory of them performing the skill from the inside and get the general sense of your role model's confidence.

6. Do this several times, until you have a strong sense of how confident it is to be your role model.

Creating our feelings...

Part of how we create our feelings is from the movies in our mind and sounds in our minds – the things we say to ourselves with our internal dialogue. All day long, we talk to ourselves with an internal voice to guide us through life, 'Oh, that looks interesting', 'I must remember to call Frank', 'Watch out, there's a bus coming', etc.

Last year, I was doing a radio interview and before we went live to air the presenter said he wanted to thank me, because he'd used one of my techniques to give himself more confidence. There was a girl he worked with who he was very attracted to, but he didn't have the confidence to ask her out. He practised changing his internal dialogue and became much more confident. Then, he added: "We've been married now for 15 years."

So, let's do a technique to increase your confidence by controlling your internal dialogue.

Your New Confident Internal Dialogue

1. Locate your internal voice. Just ask yourself, "Where is my internal voice?" and notice the location where you hear the words. At the front of your head, the back or the side.

2. Now, I would like you to imagine how your voice sounds if it is totally confident. Is it louder or softer than usual? Is it clearer and easier to hear? Is it stronger or weaker? Do you speak faster or more slowly?

    However your voice sounds when you are really positive and confident, put that voice in the same location where your old internal voice was located.

3. Now in a strong calm voice say these words over and over, "All is well, all is well, all is well," and notice how that makes you feel.

4. Next, take a few moments to think of some of the negative suggestions you have habitually given yourself in the past, things like:

"I'm shy and nervous."

"I am rubbish at giving presentations."

"I will never find someone to fall in love with me."

5. For each statement, come up with its positive opposite.

"I'm a naturally confident person."

"I always give excellent presentations."

"I am extremely loveable."

6. Finally, I want you to repeat the new, positive suggestions to yourself in your new, confident internal voice – say the new statements over and over again.

The Power of Posture

The three things that determine how we feel and act at any moment in our lives are the pictures, the sounds in our minds and also our physiology (our posture).

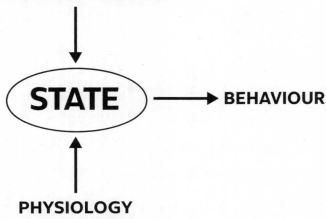

INTERNAL REPRESENTATIONS
The pictures and sounds we make in our mind and how we make them

STATE → **BEHAVIOUR**

PHYSIOLOGY
Posture, muscular tension, breathing, etc

Nobody has ever marched into my office with their head held high and exclaimed, "I'm depressed!". Those people are usually slouching and looking at the ground. When you are excited, your posture reflects that. When you are sad, your posture is different. The legendary movie star Roger Moore once told me that when he first went to acting school, he had a teacher who asked him, "How tall are you?" "6'1"" he replied. "So, why don't you stand as though you are 6'1"?" said the teacher. Roger straightened up and from that day onwards, he started getting more work.

The Golden Thread Technique

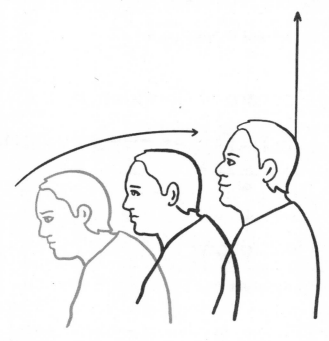

I have a simple exercise that creates this effect. I imagine that there is a golden thread coming down from the sky, going through the very top of my head and down through my core, which is holding me upright. I imagine this thread holding me up straight and taking my weight, so I am relaxed, but with a tall, upright posture. It takes just a couple of seconds to remember it, to let your body respond and to feel the benefits. It is particularly useful if you are tired or stressed or have spent too long hunched over a computer.

Use it as often as you can, and after a while you will notice that your body wants to keep that relaxed, upright posture.

The Posture of Confidence

Social psychologist Amy Cuddy of the Harvard Business School has become famous for her work showing that our posture also influences our state of mind and body. Cuddy conducted an experiment which demonstrated that both physiology and behaviour are directly affected by posture. Cuddy's subjects were not given any guidance. They were simply asked to sit or stand in specific poses – some were power poses that exude confidence and others were not. Then, they were put through a gruelling job interview. Their behaviour and performance were assessed by judges who had no information about what they had been asked to do. Subjects who had been given the power poses significantly outperformed those who had been given low status poses.

Just two minutes in the poses was enough to make significant physiological and behavioural differences. The behaviour of the power pose subjects was more confident and assertive, their levels of cortisol (the stress hormone) were lower and their levels of testosterone (the confidence hormone) were elevated.

Cuddy used three simple poses. The wonderful thing about these poses is that even when we believe our negative thoughts are unstoppable or our feelings are overwhelming, we can always simply move our limbs and take up these positions. Within two minutes of moving into these poses, our physiology and hence our whole state is changed.

I am optimistic but also sceptical, so I tested the poses myself. I felt great, but I still wasn't sure. Maybe I had just used them to boost my natural optimism. So, I turned to a close friend who had a tendency to be a bit self-effacing. The greeting on her voicemail sounded like she was apologising for existing. I didn't explain anything. I just asked her to do the poses for two minutes each. Then, I asked her to re-record her voicemail greeting. The difference was startling! Now she sounded like a chief executive.

I've shared Cuddy's amazing work with many, many friends and clients since. Some of them go to the bathroom to do the poses before important meetings (obviously, you wouldn't do them in public), and they notice that even walking from the bathroom to the meeting room people treat them differently. They exude power, authority and confidence.

I believe Amy Cuddy's work is simple, brilliant and powerful and I want you to try it right now. If you find these exercises uncomfortable or strange, or if you find yourself saying, "This is weird," then you *absolutely must* practise them until they feel as natural and comfortable as sitting in your favourite chair. If these postures feel silly, or unusual, or bad, or difficult for you, that means that for years you have been training yourself to sit or stand in low status poses. You have been telling people you are an underdog. Indirectly and unintentionally, you have been inviting people to put themselves in positions of power over you. Starting right now, you absolutely must do these power poses until they feel completely natural and comfortable.

If you already find these poses natural and easy, or if they feel familiar, that is great – you already have an excellent base for influencing others – but you will still benefit from practising them, as they will enhance your power and influence even more.

These poses are great preparation before a presentation, an interview or an important performance. If you need privacy, you can go and do them in the bathroom and do them beforehand. It's all about mental preparation.

Power Poses

POSE 1: Wonder Woman – Place your hands on your hips, stand tall with your legs apart and embrace the feeling of your inner confidence.

POSE 2: Winner –
Stand tall, with your
arms up high like a
star with your fingers
pointing skywards.

POSE 3: Boss – place your
hands behind the back of
your head, elbows wide,
in a relaxed, confident way.

For each of these poses,
do the following:

1. Hold the pose.

2. Continue to hold for two minutes.
   Observe and embrace the feeling.

3. Relax and carry on with your life
   energised and empowered.

The Negative Thought Fast...

Nearly 40 years ago, when I first started experimenting with the pictures and sounds in my mind and the effect they had on my feelings, I soon noticed as I felt so good in myself more often. It changed the way I behaved and the results I was getting in the world. My life changed immeasurably for the better. One process that I did for an entire week in particular made a significant difference to my life.

I went on a negative thought fast.

This is how it works. When we have a thought, an electrical impulse travels down a set of neural pathways in the brain. The more times it does it, the physically bigger the neural pathways becomes – just like a muscle, the more you use it, the bigger it gets. This is how people get hardwired to certain habits, such as smoking. A person feels stressed, so they fire off the electrical impulses that are associated with smoking and after a while any stress triggers a desire for a cigarette. However, it's possible to be hardwired to positive and negative things. Some people are hardwired to take exercise, feel confident in the face of a challenge, motivated every morning to go for what they want in life, or just feel good for no particular reason. And it is something that can be learned and installed into your brain, just like a new programme for a computer. Later, we will be training your brain to give you powerful motivation. Right now, let's learn one of the best ways to feel good more often – starve your mind of unnecessary negativity.

The Negative Thought Fast

1. Whenever you find yourself feeling bad about anything, stop and ask yourself what you are feeling bad about and notice what image, sound, or words come to mind.

   Remember, your emotions are signals, letting you know when you need to pay extra attention to some aspect of your experience. *Every* feeling in your body is linked to an internal picture, sound, or by the words you say to yourself in your mind. ▷

2. Listen for the message or positive intention of the emotion

Negative or uncomfortable emotions are just messengers sent by your mind and body to let you know it's time to pay attention to something. For example, if I have a worrying feeling and I stop to notice what comes to mind and, say, it's the image of an upcoming meeting, my mind is trying to alert me to things that might go wrong in that meeting and to make sure I am well prepared.

3. Act on the message!

So, in this example, I might make a list of all the things I can do to stop those problems occurring and take action on at least one of them.

4. Turn off the messenger

This is like hanging up the phone or resetting the smoke alarm. When I've heeded my mind's warning, I drain all the colour out of the image, shrink it down to the size of a postage stamp, and send it off into the distance. If the picture pops back, it's because there's still something you need to be aware of, so find out what it is.

5. Programme your desired future

Then, imagine events go exactly the way you want them to. In the example of my upcoming meeting, I make a big, bright movie of the meeting going perfectly and watch it all the way up to the conclusion.

If at any time over the next week, you find yourself feeling bad, stop and do this process – it will give your mind an opportunity to signal something to you, but it will stop the message signalling too loud and too often. This process will change the landscape of your brain chemistry by continually emphasizing the positive and not dwelling unnecessarily on the negative.

In a Nutshell

- People that are confident are comfortable in their own skin.

- The state of confidence is created by the pictures we create in our mind, our internal dialogue and our posture.

- We can increase confidence by imagining a more confident self and stepping into it.

- Confidence is a habit – the more we practise it, the better we get.

Section 3

The Easy Way to Build Resilience

Many people think that resilience is just about toughing it out, about being relentless. Whilst there is truth in that, resilience is also about adaptability and flexibility. So, resilience is really the ability to think creatively, combined with persistence.

The Law of Requisite Variety, which comes from the scientific field of Cybernetics, shows us that the system or person with the most flexibility of behaviour will control that system – that could be in a corporation, a political party, or a family. The more flexible you are when you hit a challenge, the more likely you will control your life and get what you want. In other words, it's a good strategy to generate more choices in any given situation. We can think about this another way:

The only way you can control your destiny is to be more flexible than your environment.

As a hypnotist, if a patient has seven ways of resisting my attempts to help them change, I need eight ways to convince them. The metaphor I often use is when a reed is blowing in the wind, if it's too stiff, it will snap, but if it's flexible, then it survives by adapting to the environment.

One of the most important distinctions that human beings have over animals is our imagination. If you look around you right now, most of what you see will have once been an idea in someone's imagination. The beauty of the human imagination is that it allows us to experiment with variables before we act on them. We can imagine what bacon-flavoured ice-cream would taste like before we eat it.

All the great creative geniuses throughout history made use of their imaginations in ways that others didn't, combined with perseverance. Thomas Edison's teachers said he was "too stupid to learn anything." He was fired from his first two jobs for being 'non-productive'. As an inventor, Edison made over 1,000 unsuccessful attempts at inventing the light bulb. When a reporter asked, "How did it feel to fail 1,000 times?" Edison replied, "I didn't fail 1,000 times. The light bulb was an invention with 1,000 steps." In other words, in Edison's mind each 'failure' was a step in the direction of success.

Albert Einstein came up with the Theory of Relativity by asking smarter questions than other physicists and he asked them over and over again. Over the years, I've learned that a good question is worth its weight in gold – not only for the answers it draws forth but also for the positive frame of mind it can help you get into.

One of the best techniques in helping me solve problems over the years are a set of questions that come from the field of decision theory. These six questions are brilliant at helping you to think outside the box when solving problems.
Before we use them, I want to ask you a really important question:

What are your three biggest problems?

Take all the time you need to consider what they are first. Don't try to solve them yet but next ask yourself, "What would it feel like if you knew *how* to solve them?" Then, ask yourself, "What would it feel like if you knew you were *going* to solve them?".

The Simple Perspective Shift

A few years ago, I worked with a famous comedian who had just become one of the biggest stars in America. He had been asked to host a prestigious awards ceremony and he explained that it was a daunting prospect for him. So, we did a simple but very effective technique.

I asked him to imagine his entire lifeline stretching from one side of the room to the other, so he could see it all laid out in front of him. Next, I asked him to tell me how big, in the grand scheme of his life, this event would be if we could see the size of it on the floor now. Surprised, he said, "About as thin as a slither of paper," and in that moment his perspective began to change. Suddenly, it wasn't a do-or-die experience – it became just another challenge, which he could cope with.

Albert Einstein famously said, "We cannot solve our problems with the same thinking we used when we created them."

So, let's learn how to change our perspective with some problem-solving techniques now…

Problem-Solving Questions

In order to get these questions to work for you, simply choose a problem, concern or worry and answer each question as honestly as you can.

The first question is sometimes a challenge for people because they are in the mindset of the problem and the questions are designed to help you step out of that mindset.

So, for example, if your problem is, 'I can't lose weight,' asking yourself what's positive about the problem, often brings up nothing at all, at first. However, when you start thinking outside of the problem, potential answer could be perhaps that you are not undernourished. I once did this with someone who was unwell who thought there was no possible positive about their illness. After a number of attempts, he said, "Well, at least I know what's wrong with me and I am getting treatment." Remember, the idea is not necessarily to solve the problem immediately, but to get yourself thinking about it differently.

So, think about one of your problems and then ask yourself these questions…

1. What are three positive things about this problem?

2. What's not yet the way you want it?

3. What are you willing to do to get the result you want?

4. What are you willing to stop doing to get the result you want?

5. How can you motivate yourself and even take pleasure in doing what needs to be done to get the result you want?

6. What's something you can do today to get things moving in the right direction?

Each time you ask and answer these questions, you will gain new insights into how to better handle the situation you are exploring.

Role Model Step-In

Hypnosis is often described as a 'state of deep focus' and I find that to be a helpful way to think about it. So, as a hypnotist, I often ask people to relax and focus, or imagine things going the way they want them to – for example, giving a great presentation, or living life free of the cravings for cigarettes. Sometimes, when I work with corporations, they are concerned about me doing hypnosis, because they have pre-conceived ideas that it's some kind of mind control. Personally, I believe anything that gives you more control over your mind is a good thing. However, when there is any concern about hypnosis, I simply remind people that there are many different processes in which a form of hypnosis is present. For example, in the corporate world, it could be perceived as 'strategic planning,' – i.e. when a group of executives sit and relax and imagine what their product or service will be like in the future, what challenges they may have to overcome, how they can expand their business and increase their efficiency.

Any time you focus on one thing to the exclusion of all others, it is a form of hypnosis

– when you're watching TV, you forget about the carpet, the curtains and the rest of the room. Whatever goes on on-screen, you entrain yourself to – so, if it's frightening, you get scared, or if it's a love scene, you feel romantic. In meditation, you're focussing on a mantra or your breathing, and you forget about the room you are in or the people that may be around you. All these things are a form of hypnosis or a trance-like state if you will.

The reason why we do this is when you're in a relaxed, imaginative state you can imagine doing things that are outside of the normal boundaries of possibility. So, you can imagine being really confident meeting new people or you can imagine achieving your goals. Great creative people throughout history have used this state of mind in order to visualize new possibilities. One of the greatest equations of all time is Einstein's Theory of Relativity but in order to arrive at that, he had to use his creative imagination, and he imagined what it would be like to ride on a beam of light – not something that's possible to do in real life, but something you can do in your imagination!

Sometimes the difference that makes the difference in solving problems is not just looking at the situation in a different way but looking at it with different eyes.

We have all had the experience of getting stuck with a problem and asking someone else for their opinion. They then point something out that up until that moment we had not seen and once we do see it, it becomes obvious to us.

Here's all you need to do to give yourself a whole new insight into your problems and begin generating positive solutions:

1. Think of somebody who is good at solving problems and sorting things out.

   The person you choose can be real, or they can be a character from a story. Over the years, I have seen people choose everyone from Sherlock Holmes to Elon Musk – from Bill Gates to their Aunt Gladys.

   All that matters is that you have a strong enough sense of what they are like, so that you can imagine them vividly in your mind.

2. Now, imagine stepping into your role model and take a few moments to imagine yourself seeing the world through your problem-solver's eyes. See what they would see and hear what they would hear.

3. While still looking through their eyes, think about a particular problem you have and consider it from this point of view. How would they handle it if it was their problem? What advice would they give you about it? What do they think is the best course of action?

4. Act on any insights you have!

The importance of persistence...

My first international bestseller was called 'Change Your Life In 7 Days'. I would get asked all the time in interviews, "Can you really change your life in 7 days?" To which I would reply, "You can change your life in 7 seconds." Everyone has had the experience of getting so fed up with a situation that they make a decision not to put up with that anymore and in that moment, their life changes. We've all had the experience of coming up with an idea that changes our world or meeting a particular person and our lives are never the same again.

Many of history's great successes and inventions failed or were continually rejected, but the difference between the successes and the failures was the winners just kept going until they succeeded. Bill Gates' first business failed. Jim Carrey used to be homeless. Stephen King's first novel was rejected 30 times. Jay-Z couldn't get signed to any record labels. The Beatles were rejected by every major record company. J K Rowling was rejected by publishers over and over again. Colonel Sanders' chicken recipe was rejected 1,009 times before he sold it to his first restaurant. James Dyson, the creator of the Dyson vacuum cleaner, took 5,126 attempts before he had success.

I have been doing a podcast called Positivity over the last couple of years where I do a psychological rather than journalistic interview with a well-known person. Guests have included Simon Cowell, John Cleese, Roger Daltrey, Baroness Karren Brady, Andy McNab, Pru Leith, Tony Robbins, Mel B, Paul Oakenfold, Ryan Seacrest and KSI amongst many others.

I make it a point to ask all my guests about how they manage to overcome adversity. Every one of them has really interesting stories about how the have kept going in the face of challenges. The actress Priyanka Chopra Jonas is a very inspiring lady who when facing any sort of setback, motivates herself by thinking of all her past successes, large or small, to put whatever challenge she is facing into a more empowering perspective.

This next technique will help you do just that. You can use it whenever you need to overcome feelings of desperation.

The Desperation Destroyer

1. Think about something you feel needy or desperate about. It could be money, a sale, a job, or even a relationship you would like to have.

2. Notice the pictures, sounds and self-talk you have associated to this situation.

3. Now, take charge of your internal world! Take any negative pictures, push them off into the distance in your mind's eye and fade them out. Turn down the volume on the negative sounds and self-talk until you are feeling relatively calm about whatever it is you were feeling desperate about.

4. Next, make a nine-square grid and create a 'success collage' of some of the good things you have in your life or of happy memories – putting 8 of them in the boxes, but keep the bottom middle box free for the time being. Imagine pictures of the people that you like and who like you, times where you have been successful in the past, and anything else you are grateful for having in your life.

5. Finally, in the bottom middle box, fill the space with a very tiny, black and white representation of whatever it is you used to feel needy or desperate about.

> 6. In the future, you will only think about this thing in the context of all the wonderful things you already have going for you!

Taking Control of Your Life

I remember when I started in showbusiness, somebody said to me the hardest thing you will find when you become successful is to say 'no.' At the time, I didn't really understand what they meant, but there was one day that changed my life – overnight, I became famous. I made a TV show that was one of the most watched shows in the UK that year and the next day I couldn't walk down the street without being stopped or stared at. My phone rang off the hook. It seemed like everyone wanted to interview me or wanted a photo or autograph. Prior to that, I'd been working away non-stop and struggling, so I said yes to nearly everything but then suddenly I was totally overwhelmed.

At the time, I had just finished reading *The 7 Habits of Highly Successful People* by Stephen Covey. The single most important idea I took away from that book was that rather than just try to work my way through the mountain of things that needed to be done each day, I had to create an A, B and C list.

A-list items were things that had to be done urgently or there would be trouble.

B-list items were things that were important but could wait.

Everything else was a C-list item.

I had to streamline my priorities. That way, I could get more done without feeling over-whelmed. Suddenly, my stress levels reduced and my productivity went through the roof. So, our next technique is simply this…

The ABC List Exercise

1. Write down a list of everything that is on your to-do list.

2. Assign an A to those things that are urgent and have serious consequences if you do not do them.

3. Give a B to those things that are important but can wait.

4. Give a C to everything else.

5. Every morning, assess and adjust your list and concentrate on getting the A list done as soon as you can and if you have time left, go onto the Bs, and then the Cs, in that order.

6. For the next 21 days, stick religiously to the list and notice how much more productive you are and how much calmer you are about your tasks.

Labels

As a therapist, I am reluctant to label people. There is an emphasis these days on giving people a label at school or by the psychological or psychiatric community. Some people are told they are 'not artistic'. Other people are told that they are 'depressive' or 'compulsive'. The obsession with labelling people in the area of mental health is partly down to the culture of the psychiatric community, in as much as if they can describe a disorder, then it's possible to prescribe a drug for it. The problem is that depression is now one of the fastest growing diseases in the world, partly because there are plenty of medications to 'treat' it. According to James Davis from his book *How Modern Capitalism Created the Mental Health Crisis*, nearly a quarter of the entire UK adult population is now being prescribed a psychiatric drug each year, yet there has been no reduction at all in the prevalence of mental disorders since the 1980s. This is the opposite of what you would expect if the drugs were working. What's more, recent research has shown that believing mental illness is rooted in biological abnormalities can have an adverse impact on someone's recovery. For example, according to a Harvard study published in 2020, people diagnosed with depression who believe their problems are due to chemical imbalances experience greater pessimism about their recovery, as well as more depressive symptoms after their treatment has ended.

One of my problems with a label is that it often sounds permanent and the person can take the label as their identity. So, they believe that they are broken and that they have no choice but to live with it.

However, just because someone once told you that you are 'something' doesn't mean you have to believe it and very often it can be changed. A lot of people tell me about their unhappiness and how demotivating it is. They begin by telling me their story about why they are different and why they can't change and these are the sorts of the things they had been saying to themselves:

- I don't believe I can ever be truly happy.
- I don't want to get my hopes up and be let down.
- I will never get over it.
- Nothing will make any difference.
- I've tried everything and nothing works.

If you were telling yourself those sorts of things, of course it would adversely affect you. Whilst you believe your story is real, you will look to the outside world to confirm that story. Once you can see that your story, no matter how compelling it may seem, is just the sum total of what you've been telling yourself, you open up to the possibility of making changes on the inside, that will literally change your world.

If your story says that you are defined by what you have done in the past, you will almost certainly repeat that past on into the future. If you tell yourself a new story about how it's possible to begin doing things differently in any moment, you can change your future, starting right now.

The point is this:

***What you've thought of as your limitations
are just a story you tell yourself
and you can change that story
in any moment.***

I'm now going to show you how to let go, stage by stage, of any old stories you may be telling yourself, so that your natural emotional equilibrium can return to balance.

We are going to take the major unhappy memories out of your mind and put them on an imaginary wall of very small black and white pictures and just before they disappear, see them for what they are now – just thoughts.

Letting Go of Your Negative Stories

1. Think about a situation you have been stressing and/or worrying about.

2. Now, begin to notice what you've been telling yourself about that situation.

    'There's nothing I can do to change this.'

    'I was just born this way.'

    'I've been told by an 'expert' that I can't change.'

3. Now, really hear that inner voice and notice where it is coming from. Is it the front, side or back of your head?

4. Imagine floating those words out of your head and imagine hearing those words coming from somewhere about 12 feet away from you. Hear it as if they are coming from over there now.

5. As you hear it telling you that old story from 12 feet away, notice how different it feels to hear it like that.

6. This simple difference allows your mind to recalibrate and frees you from

identifying with that story. Hearing that voice over there means that there is now room for a different story over here.

5. Now, as gradually as you like, turn down the volume of that story over there.

6. Notice that you are now free to tell yourself a new story – a story of possibility, hope, and power. You may want to write down your new story or even speak it out loud. The more you repeat your new story, the more real it will start to become for you.

In a Nutshell

- Resilience = persistence + flexibility + creative thinking.

- The only way to control your destiny is to become more flexible in your environment.

- A great way to solve problems is to think about them from many different perspectives – for example, think about somebody who is good at solving problems and step into their perspective.

- Use the ABC list to prioritize issues and free up bandwidth in your thinking for creativity.

- No matter what happens to us in life, the commentary that we add about it can either empower or disempower us – if it disempowers us, it's time to change the story.

Section 4

Motivation Power & Your Positive Future

We have just been focusing primarily on the state of confidence – that feeling in your body of being comfortable, powerful and at ease. But if all you did was to sit around all day long feeling confident, your life would not necessarily change for the better. You have to point yourself in a direction in life and then take consistent daily action to move towards what it is that you want.

So, try this experiment now...

> *Imagine we have travelled into the future, a few years before the end of your life and you never took the action you wanted to create the changes you want in your life. How do you feel? What does it inspire you to do, or not do now?*

Whatever your experience of that was, come fully back into the present.

Now, I'd like you to imagine going way off into the future again, near the end of your life, but in this future, you know exactly what you wanted and you have taken action every single day to make your life the way you want it.

How is this future different? How do you feel? What does living in this way inspire you to do, or not do now?

Take the time to really think through the changes you could make, even if they're only tiny adjustments, to get you on the road to living life as you want.

We all have things we are motivated to move towards and other things we are motivated to move away from. Some people are more 'stick', others are more 'carrot'. Both are motivators but finding out whichever combination of the two inspires you to take action is your own personal key to successful motivation.

Of course, we all have things that we need to make sure we move away from. For example, if

I don't get out of bed in the morning, I could get fired or my business might fail, so the moving away from failure is a motivation to get up. However, if we are just constantly moving away from feeling bad, in a state of continual worry or anxiety, it will be exhausting and uncomfortable, as though we are forever 'on the run.' Our bandwidth of thinking is almost solely occupied with that, so there isn't any time left for experiencing joy and happiness. That's why it's really important to have good things to move towards – things to look forward to. As Steven Spielberg revealed, some mornings he wakes up so excited, he can't eat breakfast. Now, there is someone who is moving towards what makes him feel good!

When I started writing my book 'I Can Make You Rich', I began modelling super-rich achievers such as Richard Branson, Anita Roddick and Stelios Haji-Ioannou in order to understand their success strategies and winning mindset. Early on, when I was modelling the late billionaire Sir David Barclay, he said to me that I would almost certainly meet people who were very wealthy, but not truly rich – that their overwhelming motivation was to move away from an inner fear of being poor and so they only ever temporarily got to enjoy whatever they'd achieved, because the main feelings that motivated them to create money and business success were insecurity and fear.

One of the best stories I have ever heard that explains this well comes from the writer Kurt Vonnegut: 'Joseph Heller, an important and funny writer now dead, and I were at a party given by a billionaire on Shelter Island. I said, "Joe, how does it make you feel to know that our host only yesterday may have made more money than your novel 'Catch-22' has earned in its entire history?" And Joe said, "I've got something he can never have." And I said, "What on earth could that be, Joe?" And Joe said, "The knowledge that I've got enough."' Or as Bob Marley beautifully put it, "Some people are so poor all they have is money."

It's important to know what it is that you do want and to move towards it – otherwise you end up with a life of never really feeling content, just fleeting moments of pleasure. The other reason it's important to know what it is you want is because:

You always get more of what you focus on in life

Years ago, I worked with Sir Nick Faldo, one of the world's greatest golfers who had developed a habit of hitting the ball in the bunker instead of the hole. I flew out to Florida and met him on the golf course. We looked at the pin, where the hole is way off in the distance and he lined up to take his shot, but he hit it in a completely different direction, so it landed, not just in the bunker but *perfectly in the middle of the bunker!* I asked him what went through his mind just before he took the shot and he said, "I thought to myself, 'I mustn't hit it in the bunker,' and I pictured the bunker."

So, I said, "I'd like you to try an experiment. I want you to try to NOT hit the ball in the hole." He looked at me, puzzled and said, "Why would I want to do that?" and I said, "Because when you think about NOT doing something, your unconscious mind does not process the negation. In other words, if I say, 'don't think of elephants,' you have to think of an elephant to then move the picture of it away in your mind." So, I instructed him to try to not think about hitting the ball in the hole and bam! Straightaway, he hit the ball right next to the hole. The very next day he hit a-hole-in-one!

Far too often, people tell me what they *don't* want – they *don't* want to be overweight, they *don't* want to be frightened, they *don't* want to be awake all night long, they *don't* want to procrastinate. They are focusing way too much on what they *don't* want, rather than what they *do* want. Most people spend more time making a list for what they want from the supermarket each week, than on what they really want to achieve in the next five years of their lives. My friend Michael Neill, the renowned success coach says, "If you just tell a lamppost your plans every day, they are more likely to happen."

However, some people are just not sure about what it is they really want in life, or how they're going to achieve it. In that case, the best way to get clear about what it is that you really want is to get in touch with your core values.

Core Values

There's an old saying that goes, 'Too many people end up cured of their therapist's problems.' In other words, the therapist often unintentionally tries to install their model of happiness in their patient and if the therapist and patient have different values, that's where an inner conflict in their life's direction can arise. In the same way, far too many people end up doing things that maybe their parents wanted for them, or things that their friends and peers aimed for. The best way to avoid this problem is to get clear about your core values before you ever design your goals, because you or your unconscious mind is ultimately the expert on *you*.

So, what we are going to do next is to get you clear about your core values.

Before you even think about making any goals, it is very important to get really clear about what's most important to you in life. In other words, your values have to come first. For example, some people say, "I'd like to have lots of money." But if I ask, "What will that give you, or get for you?" Often, the desire for lots of money stems back to wanting a feeling of security – always having enough food on the table, not having to worry about a mortgage, etc. So, their actual value is *security* – not bits of green paper. Values are those things that are most important to us in life and we can easily make a list of between 5-10.

I remember once working with a man who said to me that he wanted a big house, a car and a boat. So, I asked him, "When you think about achieving that, how do you look?" He said, "I haven't thought about that." So, I asked, "Are you prepared to work yourself to death to get all this stuff?" In actual fact, he also wanted the time and the health to enjoy these things. Therefore, in your list of values, you should make sure you have 'being healthy and happy', because without your health, there's little point to physical possessions or monetary wealth.

Knowing Your Values

So, ask yourself, "What is most important to me?" For example, it could be your family, your career, fame, money, health or relationships.

Choose the five most important things in your life. Take each one in turn and ask yourself, "What it is it about this that is important to me?" For example, if money is important to you ask, "What is it about money that is important to me?" The answer might be 'security,' or 'status,' or 'freedom.' That would show you that the values which are important to you are security, status and freedom. If family is important to you, ask yourself, "What is important to me about my family?" The answer might be 'enjoying their company.' Ask again, "What is important about that?" and the answer might be 'love,' 'companionship,' 'connection.'

Keep asking, "What is it about this that is important to me?" until you reach the value that drives it.

Go through each of your most important things and write a list of all the values that underpin them. These are your core values.

Years ago, I used to be a relentless goal-setter. Don't get me wrong, having goals is great, however, all I seemed to have in my life was an endless list of goals that I hadn't reached as yet. I would decide that I was going to achieve a certain thing by a certain date and then get consumed with that goal. Indeed, having these goals did help me become good at achieving things, but the cost was I would get utterly frustrated if I didn't achieve exactly what I wanted when I wanted to. If things didn't turn out exactly the way I wanted, I'd be left feeling empty. My life felt like one long, endless quest. Then, one day, it struck me that I was on a never-ending drive to have more stuff, more money, more power, more status, more fame and there would never be an end to it and I'd never be satisfied.

So, I made a simple, but powerful shift in my perception. I went over to living my life first and foremost in conjunction with my values, as opposed to just for achievement and pleasure.

Unless happiness is the backdrop to our lives, life will always be an uphill slog. The good thing is happiness is always there – you just need to know how to look.

And that's where your values become so important, because a value-driven life is where real happiness comes from. There's a difference between happiness and pleasure. Pleasure comes from things like a glass of champagne, buying a new car, a nice holiday. Happiness is when we're living life in tune with our values – it's the backdrop to our lives, rather than just momentary spikes of pleasure.

So, for me personally, health is my number one value. If I feel physically and mentally healthy then I can tick that box. My other values are things such as love. Do I feel loved? Was I loving to my family and friends today? Am I being creative? Am I attempting to make a difference in the world? If I can tick those boxes every day to say that I am living my life in conjunction with my values, then, I'm living a happy life.

Overcoming Self-Sabotage

I have very rarely worked with a person who is lazy. Most of the so-called 'lazy' people I meet are actually suffering from procrastination and procrastinators are usually just frightened to make the wrong choice. They're terrified of making a wrong decision, so they do nothing. What they don't realize is 'doing nothing' is technically a choice in itself.

When someone feels a desire to go for a goal, but is also frightened of failing, it creates an internal conflict. It's a bit like driving down the street with one foot on the accelerator and the other slamming on the brake at the same time. Another way of describing this internal conflict would be when we think to ourselves, 'a part of me wants to go to the party with my friends but another part of me just wants to stay at home to veg out on the sofa with a box set.' We may desire both options, but they are in conflict.

Some people really want to go to the gym to exercise, but another part of them can't be bothered or is embarrassed about how they think they will look in public. Both 'parts' have a positive intent but are going about fulfilling their positive intent in different ways, thus creating the internal conflict.

My friend Dr Richard Bandler has created a fabulous technique for resolving this internal conflict. I never ceased to be amazed at how this deceptively simple technique can align, in just minutes, different aspects of a person's psyche so that they operate in unison and suddenly propel them in the direction they want in life.

I once did this technique with a young woman, who couldn't commit to a relationship, flitted from job-to-job and had no clear direction. Months later, she was in a happy relationship with a thriving business and had a dynamic sense of purpose. I could give you a hundred different examples of a similar extremity of life change that has come about from using this deceptively simple technique that works on aligning at the subconscious level all the parts of the self.

So, if you ever self-sabotage, or feel blocked, or just sense that you are not totally focused, then this technique is for you...

Read through this technique first, so you know all the steps that are involved, or download the audio version and I will walk you through it.

The Easy Way to Stop Self-Sabotage

1. Identify the two conflicting beliefs or positions you have within your mind. For example, part of you wants a relationship, but another part of you might want to stop you having a relationship because it believes that it will keep you safe from being hurt. If that part is scared you will fail and feel upset, it may sabotage your attempts to succeed, to get it over with and minimize the pain. Pick whatever issue you feel conflicted about internally.

2. Place your hands out in front of you with your palms facing up. Imagine the part that has the exciting positive intent for you in your dominant hand and the more cautious, 'keep-you-safe,' part in your other hand.

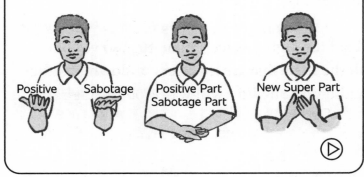

Positive   Sabotage   Positive Part   New Super Part
Sabotage Part

3. Ask each part in turn what its positive intention is for you in wanting what it wants. Continue asking until you recognize that at some level, they both want the same thing – for you to feel good and for your life to work. Even · if it feels like you are just making it up, going through this process will create dramatic changes in your levels of confidence and self-belief

So, in the 'wanting a relationship' example...

The exciting, positive intent could be:

The experience of love = having a partner = have a fulfilling life = SUCCESS!

And the sabotage, 'keep you safe' part could be:

Prevent intimacy = prevent pain = safety = SUCCESS!

4. Now, bring your hands together and let your unconscious mind figure out how these two parts can work together to give you the positive things that both parts want. It may take a few moments before you feel that they both just click.

5. Once you feel they can work together, bring your hands into your chest and take the new integrated part inside you.

6. Now, imagine being able to do the things you want free of self-sabotage but with all the protection you need.

This technique is used with the written permission of Dr Richard Bandler.

As you practise this technique, you will find it becomes easier and easier to resolve every internal conflict in this way and when all the parts of yourself are aligned and moving in the same direction, you will have become focused like a laser beam on whatever you decide to do!

The importance of direction

As Goethe, one of the all-time foremost thinkers famously said, "The greatest thing in this world is not so much where we stand as in what direction we are moving." So, rather than only having hard, fixed goals, these days, I have a clear idea of the direction of my life with some goals along the way and my wish for you is that you do, too. Everything we've been doing will help you build a clearer direction for your life that will fill you with a sense of purpose and motivation every day. You will have a truly compelling future.

The late Anita Roddick, the creator of The Body Shop once said to me that she'd never met a super successful person who took risks. She explained: "They all took educated, calculated risks." So, before we design your compelling future and get you highly motivated, I'd like to show you a method that the high achievers use to make good decisions.

Taking risks is a necessary part of achieving anything in life, but there's a difference between calculated risks and reckless risks. Professional risk-takers such as Richard Branson go through a process of evaluation before they make a business decision.

Or to put it another way, one of my friends who is a super successful businessman has what he calls an 'intuitive approach' to making business decisions – his decisions are ultimately gut instinct. Having observed a number of successful people who work mostly on gut instinct, there is still a process their mind goes through. I have noticed their strategy is to first gather lots of information, through observation and intelligent questions, asking about why something should work or what could get in the way. They then let their minds percolate all the pros and cons before they get their 'gut feeling' to reach a decision about what to do. So, ultimately, it's a strategy of evaluation and like any strategy, they started out practising it step-by-step, until eventually it becomes unconscious or second nature.

My friend Dr Stephen Simpson has made a remarkable study of intuition. This comes from his work with some of the world's leading poker players. When he works with them, on average their winnings increase tenfold. Poker is a game of statistics, but it is also the ability to read the other players, then, make a decision based on lots of different pieces of information to win. More generally, in life, we have a massive amount of information from our sensory awareness – pictures, sounds, smells, etc. Our mind collates this and offers us an opportunity to make a decision in the form of a gut instinct or intuition.

This is historically a survival mechanism that would alert us through an instinctive feeling about danger and would also drive us towards opportunity. However, since human beings have learned to speak, they have to some extent learned to ignore this and to also let the ego get in the way, because the ego's purpose is to look good and be right. However, as Dr Simpson suggests, when we get quiet and free ourselves of distractions such as our mobile phones and the internet, and tune into what our intuition is telling us, we will be right most of the time. Just as he is able to help leading poker players increase their earnings by making good intuitive decisions, you will find that you can do the same in life generally.

Next, is a technique that requires you to think through the upside and downside of an opportunity before you make a decision. The first few times you do this technique, you will have to really think through the steps, until eventually it becomes second nature and you will have trained you brain to make better decisions.

For example, the first time you learned to tie your shoelaces you really had to think about it, then after you had done it a number of times, it became automatic – you stored the habit or 'programme' in your unconscious mind. Making decisions based on a clean, rational, educated risk evaluation basis is what the professional risk-taker and the super achievers do. So, in a moment, we are going to practise a technique that will quickly help you learn their approach until it becomes second nature to you.

Here's how it works – think about taking a risk – such as a new business venture or asking someone out on a date. Now, it's important to consider the upside and the downside and rate them both on a scale of 1 – 10. Even though it's a simple process, long term this is a game changer.

For example, let's consider a business opportunity – when you think through the downside, let's say there is a real chance of losing quite a bit of money, so the downside is say, an 8 or 9. However, if it works, you could make a lot of money, so the upside is a 10. Whenever you have downside and upside numbers that are close then, it's clearly NOT a risk worth taking. So, you may want to re-evaluate your strategy, or even walk away from this 'opportunity'.

Now, let's say you want to ask somebody out on a date and you look at the downside and upside. There is a chance they might reject you. You would feel upset, but you'll soon get over it, so the downside is let's say a 3. However, if they say 'yes' you could have an amazing relationship and a wonderful life together, so the upside is a 10. So, when the downside is low and the upside is high, it's time to TAKE MASSIVE ACTION!

Some people only downside/upside with big decisions at first, but as you do this more and more often, soon your unconscious mind will learn the pattern of evaluation and you will be making smart decisions about everything.

Now you know how this process works, let's apply it to the major areas of your life and train your brain to think even smarter...

Take time now to think about the biggest decisions you are likely to take in the near future in these areas of your life:

1. Health
2. Relationships
3. Career

For the next seven days, please use this evaluation process whenever you make a significant decision and soon it will become second nature. You will have a kind of instant intuition.

Next, let's create a direction for your life – a compelling future!

Choices

One of the simplest ways to motivate yourself is to actually make a decision. Choice is one of the most powerful things we have as human beings. Sure, some choices are tough and some require thinking about the consequences before you make them, but in any moment, you can decide to do something different, you can choose a better path in life. As Tony Robbins says, "It's in your moments of decision that your destiny is shaped." Sometimes, when I am asking someone to imagine a better life, they say to me things such as, "I just can't see myself doing that," which tells you everything. They need a little help visualising a better life.

Or people tell me that they don't feel enough motivation. So, let's programme your mind right now to see, hear and feel a better future for you.

Creating your future now

Read through the instructions first or even better let me guide you through this process by downloading the audio version of this technique.

1. Imagine it's a year in the future and you have had one of the best years of your life.

What has happened with regard to your **health**, *mental and physical...* **relationships**, *personal and professional...* **career**... **finances**... **spiritual life**... *and your levels of* **happiness**? *How does it feel to be living your values? Which of your goals have you achieved? Which ones have you made significant progress towards? What new thinking and behaviours have you practised? Who are you becoming?*

2. Now, create an ideal scene that represents all that you most want to happen in your positive future. Make

sure you can see yourself in that future picture looking healthy, positive and happy. It can be realistic or symbolic (some people see a picture of themselves in a particular setting, looking a certain way – other people go for something more symbolic, like picturing clinking champagne glasses, celebrating a business deal, or a certificate of achievement on the wall).

For example, when I did this with a patient recently, he made an image of himself healthy and happy at a party with his family and friends. They were all sitting around celebrating his latest success at work. There was an incredible sense of prosperity about them.

What he really enjoyed about the picture was that he seemed so grounded and happy in himself.

Design your 'ideal scene' now.
Where are you?
Who are you with?
Which successes are you most aware of?
What do you like about it most?
How happy do you look?

3. So, when you have made that image one year from now, make sure the image is big, bright, bold and colourful, the size of a cinema screen. You'll know you're doing it right because it feels really good just to imagine it.

4. Next, float back three months from your big picture and ask yourself what needs to happen three months before that to achieve your big goals a year from now and make a picture that represents it. You may know straightaway, or you may just get a sense of what needs to happen. Make a picture that represents that.

Next, float back another three months from that picture and ask yourself what would need to happen three months prior to that?

Then, float back another three months from your last picture and ask yourself what needs to happen three months before that?

And make a new image that represents that.

Once again, float back three months from your last picture to now and then ask yourself what needs to happen from this day forward?

So, you are right back to now and you should be able to see a succession of images that show you the direction of your life over the next year.

5. Next, make all the images much bigger, brighter, bolder and more solid until they feel amazing.

You should now have a succession of pictures connecting the present with your positive, compelling future. The images should get progressively bigger with better and better things happening in them.

Look at those pictures and let your unconscious mind lock in the road map to your success over the next year.

6. Now, float up and out of your body and into each picture, moving forwards in time through the year. Take a few moments to fully experience each step you will be taking on the path to greater success.

7. When you get to the big picture of your ideal scene, really allow yourself to enjoy experiencing it fully. What will it be like to have everything you want?

8. Finally, come back to the present and look out once again at your future timeline. You can feel confident in the knowledge that you have now created a map for your unconscious mind to use as a guide in bringing about the future you want to create!

You should now be feeling very optimistic and motivated when you think about your future. It's important to do this process regularly and focus upon the future you want to have, look at your timeline and the succession of images of you succeeding and achieving.

As Goethe said, "A whole stream of events issues from the decision, raising in one's favour all manner of unforeseen incidents and meetings and material assistance, which no man could have dreamed would have come his way. Whatever you can do, or dream you can do, begin it."

How to increase your luck

I wanted to finish this book on a high – a really upbeat note.

My friend Roger Daltrey often says, "Be lucky." We had a conversation about this one day and he said to me that he believes that if you *think* lucky, you *are* lucky. Interestingly, the scientific research supports this. Two very clever scientists that I know, Dr Dean Radin and Dr Richard Wiseman have both independently researched luck and their findings are that some people are disproportionately luckier than others and that this is linked to their beliefs and their mindset. Put simply, people that believe they are lucky are luckier than those who believe they are unlucky.

A few years ago, I was watching a very old interview with Keith Richards of The Rolling Stones. The interviewer asked if he knew that there was a celebrity death list (famous people most likely to die young). As he casually sat there, smoking a cigarette, he asked, "Am I on it?". The interviewer replied, "Actually, you're top of the list." He took another drag on his cigarette and said, "I'll let you know how I get on. My luck hasn't run out yet." In that moment, I had this realization that luck might not be fixed – maybe it's a form of energy and our thinking and perceptions may be able to change our luck.

So, I devised a technique to help people enhance their luck. Just like any neuro-physiological state that you want to generate, remembering times when you felt lucky will recall that state. Giving the feeling a colour and making that colour brighter and bolder will amplify the state.

I taught this technique to a number of people who did it every day for a week and every one of them found that their luck changed for the better.

In a moment, we are going to do a simple visualisation technique where you remember times that you either felt lucky or that everything was going your way.

Increase your luck

1. Remember a time or times when you felt lucky. Remember them vividly, like you are back there again now. Or if you don't feel particularly lucky at the moment, remember a time in your past when you felt everything was going your way. See what you saw, hear what you heard, and feel how good you felt.

2. Now, make the images in your mind, the memory of the images, bigger, the colours brighter, bolder, richer, the sounds, louder and the feelings stronger.

3. Keep going through the memories again and again, over and over until you feel really, really good!

4. Now, notice where you feel the good feeling strongest in your body; in your chest, heart or wherever.

5. Now imagine the really good feeling has a colour and spread that colour up to the top of your head and down to the tip of your toes. Take time to do it now...

6. Next, double the brightness and intensity of the colour and feeling and double it again and again, until you feel it in every fibre of your being!

7. Now, take the colour and feeling to its absolute maximum, 100%.

8. Now take it to 120%, 130%, 140%.

9. Now take it to a million, billion, trillion % stronger. Make the colour bright bold and the feeling strong.

10. While you have that amazing feeling at a strong level, imagine spreading it to every area of your life, send your luck energy in to your health... career... relationships, personal and professional, imagine sending it into your finances and way off into your future.

Right now, you should be glowing with good feelings and positive luck energy. Do this technique every day for a week and notice how your life changes for the better.

In a Nutshell

- It's important to be clear about what it is you want in life and to design your goals from your deepest core values.

- Before you make any decision, work out the upside and downside.

- When designing your future, imagine a point in the future when everything in your life is really working well and then, working backwards, ask yourself what the steps were that you took to create that.

- Doing the Luck Exercise will help you to create a perspective whereby you see more opportunities.

A final note from Paul...

When I finished my last book, I thought that I wouldn't need to write any more. Then, the pandemic happened and I found my techniques were in demand everywhere. What I do is no longer a luxury, it has become a necessity. You should by now be feeling significantly better after having used the system in this book. Even if only one exercise has made a change for you, then I believe it's worthwhile. Please continue to use these techniques and create an amazing life for yourself. Until we meet...

Paul McKenna, London, 2021

Section 5
Gratitude Journal

The Gratitude Journal

One of the simplest and most powerful things you can do to elevate the base line of your mood is a daily gratitude journal. It really struck me how well this process works during the pandemic, when people I knew who were feeling a bit low simply made a list of everything they are grateful for and it gave them a fresh perspective. It can be big things like health, friends and family, or small things like the first cup of tea or coffee in the morning.

When you start to consider all the things that you feel grateful for, you are re-enforcing in your mind things that make you feel great. Of course, we get more of what we focus on, so you are training your brain to focus on and search out things that improve your mood. It takes just a few minutes to do each day and then if you are feeling a bit low, just read back through your lists and you will start to feel better.

As with any new habit, you have to push yourself to do it the first few times and then it becomes second nature. That's why the last section of this book contains a 30-day gratitude journal. All you have to do is make a note of 10 things that you feel grateful for – it can be the same or similar every day because the point is to elicit positive feelings connected to your life and re-enforce the good feelings. You remember how we become hardwired through what we continually think about, that's how this approach to journaling works.

Also, it's vitally important for human beings to have a sense of purpose in life. The legendary psychiatrist Victor Frankel famously said, "Purpose is the cornerstone of good mental health." Your purpose is not necessarily your job, although your work is likely to be a part of your purpose. When I was helping people during the pandemic who had lost their job, I would ask them what their purpose was. For many, it was to be a good spouse, or to be a force for good in the world, or it could just be to strive to be the best version of yourself.

So, also on your gratitude list, it is really important for you to state your purpose. You may have more than one. It may also be your purpose for that day, that week or indeed your life. I cannot emphasise enough how powerful this process is. Here's an example of my gratitude list for a day.

1. Health, mental/physical.
2. Family.
3. Friends.
4. A happy home.
5. My work.
6. First cup of tea in the morning.
7. A TV show I am looking forward to watching.
8. Where I live in the world.
9. Food and wine.
10. Clean water.

My purpose:
To be a good husband and friend.
To be creative.
To help others.
To have success in my career.

Now, it's your turn. Set aside a time each day to remember what you are grateful for and make sure to re-read your list regularly.

DAY 1

10 things that I feel grateful for today...

1. _____

2. _____

3. _____

4. _____

5. _____

6. _____

7. _____

8. _____

9. _____

10. _____

My purpose tomorrow is:

_____

_____

_____

_____

_____

_____

DAY 2

10 things that I feel grateful for today...

1. _____
2. _____
3. _____
4. _____
5. _____
6. _____
7. _____
8. _____
9. _____
10. _____

My purpose tomorrow is:

_____
_____
_____
_____
_____
_____

DAY 3

10 things that I feel grateful for today...

1. _____
2. _____
3. _____
4. _____
5. _____
6. _____
7. _____
8. _____
9. _____
10. _____

My purpose tomorrow is:

_____

_____

_____

_____

_____

_____

DAY 4

10 things that I feel grateful for today...

1. _____
2. _____
3. _____
4. _____
5. _____
6. _____
7. _____
8. _____
9. _____
10. _____

My purpose tomorrow is:

_____

_____

_____

_____

_____

_____

DAY 5

10 things that I feel grateful for today...

1. _____
2. _____
3. _____
4. _____
5. _____
6. _____
7. _____
8. _____
9. _____
10. _____

My purpose tomorrow is:

_____
_____
_____
_____
_____
_____
_____

DAY 6

10 things that I feel grateful for today...

1. _____
2. _____
3. _____
4. _____
5. _____
6. _____
7. _____
8. _____
9. _____
10. _____

My purpose tomorrow is:

_____

_____

_____

_____

_____

_____

DAY 7

10 things that I feel grateful for today...

1. _____

2. _____

3. _____

4. _____

5. _____

6. _____

7. _____

8. _____

9. _____

10. _____

My purpose tomorrow is:

_____

_____

_____

_____

_____

_____

_____

DAY 8

10 things that I feel grateful for today...

1. _____
2. _____
3. _____
4. _____
5. _____
6. _____
7. _____
8. _____
9. _____
10. _____

My purpose tomorrow is:

_____

_____

_____

_____

_____

_____

DAY 9

10 things that I feel grateful for today...

1. _____
2. _____
3. _____
4. _____
5. _____
6. _____
7. _____
8. _____
9. _____
10. _____

My purpose tomorrow is:

_____

_____

_____

_____

_____

_____

DAY 10

10 things that I feel grateful for today...

1. _____
2. _____
3. _____
4. _____
5. _____
6. _____
7. _____
8. _____
9. _____
10. _____

My purpose tomorrow is:

_____

_____

_____

_____

_____

_____

DAY 11

10 things that I feel grateful for today...

1. _____
2. _____
3. _____
4. _____
5. _____
6. _____
7. _____
8. _____
9. _____
10. _____

My purpose tomorrow is:

_____
_____
_____
_____
_____
_____
_____

DAY 12

10 things that I feel grateful for today...

1. _____
2. _____
3. _____
4. _____
5. _____
6. _____
7. _____
8. _____
9. _____
10. _____

My purpose tomorrow is:

_____

_____

_____

_____

_____

_____

DAY 13

10 things that I feel grateful for today...

1. _____
2. _____
3. _____
4. _____
5. _____
6. _____
7. _____
8. _____
9. _____
10. _____

My purpose tomorrow is:

_____
_____
_____
_____
_____
_____

DAY 14

10 things that I feel grateful for today…

1. _____
2. _____
3. _____
4. _____
5. _____
6. _____
7. _____
8. _____
9. _____
10. _____

My purpose tomorrow is:

_____

_____

_____

_____

_____

_____

DAY 15

10 things that I feel grateful for today...

1. _____
2. _____
3. _____
4. _____
5. _____
6. _____
7. _____
8. _____
9. _____
10. _____

My purpose tomorrow is:

_____

_____

_____

_____

_____

_____

DAY 16

10 things that I feel grateful for today...

1. _____
2. _____
3. _____
4. _____
5. _____
6. _____
7. _____
8. _____
9. _____
10. _____

My purpose tomorrow is:

_____
_____
_____
_____
_____
_____
_____

DAY 17

10 things that I feel grateful for today...

1. _____
2. _____
3. _____
4. _____
5. _____
6. _____
7. _____
8. _____
9. _____
10. _____

My purpose tomorrow is:

_____
_____
_____
_____
_____
_____

DAY 18

10 things that I feel grateful for today...

1. _____
2. _____
3. _____
4. _____
5. _____
6. _____
7. _____
8. _____
9. _____
10. _____

My purpose tomorrow is:

_____

_____

_____

_____

_____

_____

DAY 19

10 things that I feel grateful for today...

1. _____
2. _____
3. _____
4. _____
5. _____
6. _____
7. _____
8. _____
9. _____
10. _____

My purpose tomorrow is:

_____

_____

_____

_____

_____

_____

DAY 20

10 things that I feel grateful for today...

1. _____
2. _____
3. _____
4. _____
5. _____
6. _____
7. _____
8. _____
9. _____
10. _____

My purpose tomorrow is:

_____

_____

_____

_____

_____

_____

DAY 21

10 things that I feel grateful for today...

1. _____
2. _____
3. _____
4. _____
5. _____
6. _____
7. _____
8. _____
9. _____
10. _____

My purpose tomorrow is:

_____
_____
_____
_____
_____
_____

DAY 22

10 things that I feel grateful for today...

1. _____
2. _____
3. _____
4. _____
5. _____
6. _____
7. _____
8. _____
9. _____
10. _____

My purpose tomorrow is:

_____
_____
_____
_____
_____
_____
_____

DAY 23

10 things that I feel grateful for today…

1. _____
2. _____
3. _____
4. _____
5. _____
6. _____
7. _____
8. _____
9. _____
10. _____

My purpose tomorrow is:

_____
_____
_____
_____
_____
_____

DAY 24

10 things that I feel grateful for today…

1. _____
2. _____
3. _____
4. _____
5. _____
6. _____
7. _____
8. _____
9. _____
10. _____

My purpose tomorrow is:

_____
_____
_____
_____
_____
_____

DAY 25

10 things that I feel grateful for today...

1. _____
2. _____
3. _____
4. _____
5. _____
6. _____
7. _____
8. _____
9. _____
10. _____

My purpose tomorrow is:

_____
_____
_____
_____
_____
_____

DAY 26

10 things that I feel grateful for today...

1. _____
2. _____
3. _____
4. _____
5. _____
6. _____
7. _____
8. _____
9. _____
10. _____

My purpose tomorrow is:

_____
_____
_____
_____
_____
_____

DAY 27

10 things that I feel grateful for today...

1. _____
2. _____
3. _____
4. _____
5. _____
6. _____
7. _____
8. _____
9. _____
10. _____

My purpose tomorrow is:

_____
_____
_____
_____
_____
_____
_____

DAY 28

10 things that I feel grateful for today...

1. _____
2. _____
3. _____
4. _____
5. _____
6. _____
7. _____
8. _____
9. _____
10. _____

My purpose tomorrow is:

_____
_____
_____
_____
_____
_____

DAY 29

10 things that I feel grateful for today...

1. _____
2. _____
3. _____
4. _____
5. _____
6. _____
7. _____
8. _____
9. _____
10. _____

My purpose tomorrow is:

_____
_____
_____
_____
_____
_____
_____

DAY 30

10 things that I feel grateful for today…

1. _____
2. _____
3. _____
4. _____
5. _____
6. _____
7. _____
8. _____
9. _____
10. _____

My purpose tomorrow is:

_____
_____
_____
_____
_____
_____

Acknowledgements

My profound thanks to the following people who have helped me make this book possible, my wonderful wife Kate McKenna, Caroline Michel, Ajda Vucicevic, Marcus Leaver, Amy Brazier, Sarah Arnold, Steve Crabb, Michael Neill, Dr Stephen Simpson, Mike Osborne, Neil Reading, Dr Richard Bandler and Dr Ronald Ruden.

I would also like to thank all the thousands of people who have helped me perfect this system by allowing me to practise it on them over the last 18 months.